RIHANNA

A Little Golden Book® Biography

By Regina Andreoni • Illustrated by Laura Freeman

🌼 A GOLDEN BOOK • NEW YORK

Golden Books
An imprint of Random House Children's Books
A division of Penguin Random House LLC
1745 Broadway, New York, NY 10019
penguinrandomhouse.com
rhcbooks.com

Library of Congress Control Number: 2024945615
ISBN 978-0-593-90010-9 (trade) — ISBN 978-0-593-90011-6 (ebook)
Manufactured in the United States of America
10 9 8 7 6 5 4 3 2 1
EU Contact: Penguin Random House Ireland, 32 Nassau Street, Dublin D02 YH68.
https://eu-contact.penguin.ie.

Robyn Rihanna Fenty was born on February 20, 1988, on the island of Barbados, a country in the Caribbean. She grew up in a small house close to the beach. Her mom worked hard as an accountant to support her family. Robyn helped out by looking after her two younger brothers.

As a child, Robyn was quiet and shy. Classmates at school made fun of her for having lighter skin than them. When she felt sad, she listened to music to make herself happy. She loved singing along to Mariah Carey, Janet Jackson, and Madonna. She also enjoyed listening to Bob Marley, a reggae artist from Jamaica, another Caribbean island near Barbados.

From the ages of eleven to sixteen, Robyn was in the Barbados Cadet Corps, a volunteer program for kids to train for the military.

One of her drill sergeants—older cadets who help train the younger ones—was named Shontelle. She challenged Robyn by making her do a lot of push-ups.

During high school, Robyn competed in a beauty pageant and sang a Mariah Carey song for her talent performance. When the crowd cheered, she knew she wanted to be a professional singer. The judges were as impressed as the audience—Robyn won the competition!

Robyn formed a music group with two friends.
They sang everywhere they could, even on the beach.

Soon, the girls got a lucky break! They sang for
Evan Rogers, an American music producer who
was on vacation in Barbados. Robyn stood out from
the rest of the group. Her unique voice and style
impressed Rogers, so he invited her to his music
studio in New York.

Robyn was only sixteen years old when she flew to the United States with her mom to start her music career. Rogers helped her make a demo tape of songs to share with other producers in the music industry.

Robyn decided to release her music under her middle name, Rihanna.

It wasn't long before rapper and producer Jay-Z heard Rihanna's tape. He liked the song "Pon de Replay" and asked to hear her sing it in person.

Rihanna was nervous when she arrived at Jay-Z's office. She wanted to be a singer more than anything, and this was her big chance.

As soon as Jay-Z heard her sing, he knew Rihanna was going to be a star. Before she left that night, Rihanna had signed a six-album record deal with Jay-Z's Def Jam Recordings!

Rihanna's first album, *Music of the Sun*, debuted in 2005 when she was seventeen years old. It gained a lot of attention for its unique sound, inspired by her Caribbean roots. "Pon de Replay" was her first single from the album—and her first hit!

Less than one year later, her second album, *A Girl Like Me*, did even better. It had three top ten hits with the songs "SOS," "Unfaithful," and "Break It Off."

Rihanna kept pushing herself in the recording studio. She worked with different producers to create new sounds and lively dance music. Her albums, music videos, and concerts established her as one of the biggest singers in the world. In 2007, she won her first Grammy Award for the song "Umbrella."

Rihanna released
seven albums in
seven years. She
teamed up with
other singers, too,
including Shakira,
Drake, and Eminem.

She even reunited with Shontelle, her friend and drill sergeant from Barbados who also became a singer. Together, they wrote the hit "Man Down." The song went double platinum, which means it sold more than two million copies!

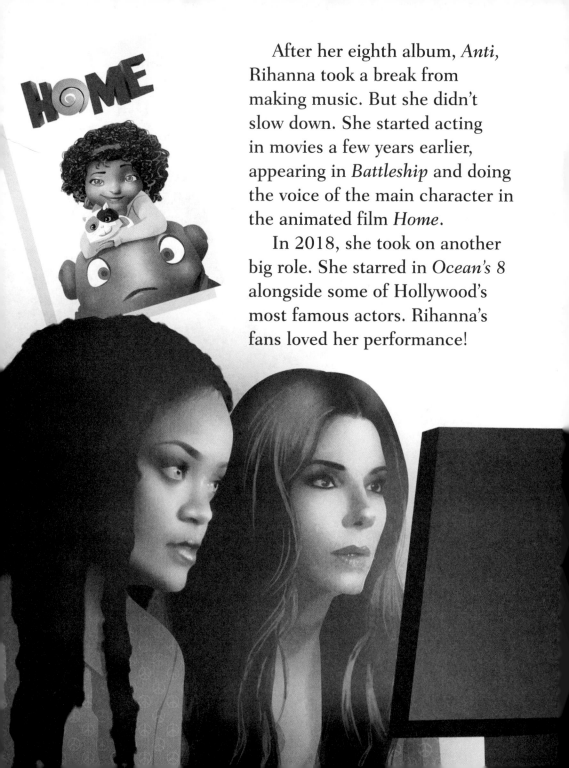

After her eighth album, *Anti*, Rihanna took a break from making music. But she didn't slow down. She started acting in movies a few years earlier, appearing in *Battleship* and doing the voice of the main character in the animated film *Home*.

In 2018, she took on another big role. She starred in *Ocean's 8* alongside some of Hollywood's most famous actors. Rihanna's fans loved her performance!

Rihanna went on to pursue other projects she was passionate about. She started her own record label, Westbury Road Entertainment, named after the street she grew up on in Barbados. She began releasing her own music under this label in 2015.

In 2017, she launched Fenty Beauty, a cosmetics company that was the first to create makeup for a wide range of skin colors, with over forty different shades.

Next came Rihanna's fashion lines, Savage X Fenty and Fenty. She designed everything from underwear and pajamas to glamorous gowns.

Her makeup brand and clothing line are for people of all skin colors and body types. Rihanna believes everyone should feel beautiful and confident.

In addition to singing and acting, Rihanna is also known for being a style icon. She loves experimenting with new looks and wearing one-of-a-kind outfits, especially at fancy events like the annual Met Gala at New York City's Metropolitan Museum of Art.

Rihanna's success allows her to help the people of Barbados. She founded the Clara Lionel Foundation in honor of her grandparents Clara and Lionel Braithwaite. It works to improve education and healthcare on the island and helps people prepare for hurricanes and other natural disasters.

In 2022, Rihanna and her long-time partner, rapper A$AP Rocky, decided to start a family. Becoming a mother was a dream come true. Nothing makes her happier than seeing her children smile.

In 2023, Rihanna performed at the Super Bowl halftime show. More than 120 million people tuned in to see her sing live for the first time in seven years. It became the most watched halftime show ever!

Rihanna sang twelve of her biggest songs, including "We Found Love" and "Only Girl (in the World)." She performed on a floating stage above the crowd and had nearly three hundred backup dancers as part of the show.

Rihanna wanted to be a star ever since she was a child singing on the beach in Barbados. Thanks to her unique style and a lot of hard work, she achieved her dreams. Fans around the globe can't wait to see what the singer, actress, entrepreneur, and fashion icon does next!